Old Peking Revisited

Old Peking Revisited

Published by:
FormAsia Books Limited
706, Yu Yuet Lai Building
45, Wyndham Street
Central, Hong Kong
www.formasiabooks.com

Published 2004
Printed in Hong Kong
ISBN 962-7283-69-X (10)
© Text FormAsia Books Limited
Photographs from The Pageant of Peking by
Donald Mennie

Written by Nigel Cameron
Digital Artwork Kitty Chan
Calligraphy, Illustrations Ian Leung
FormAsia Marketing Eliza Lee

Printed by Sing Cheong Printing Company Limited
Film separations by Sky Art Graphic Co., Limited

While every effort has been made to trace and
acknowledge copyright holders, FormAsia Books
apologizes should there be any error or omission.

Nigel Cameron

FormAsia

Donald Mennie (d.1942)

Donald Mennie was an American or British businessman based in Shanghai. He was also an amateur photographer of great accomplishment, managing to take hundreds of fascinating, technically accomplished photographs despite his hectic schedule as a Director of the well-known British pharmacists A.S. Watson & Company. We know that his work did not suffer however, because under his leadership A.S. Watson expanded greatly in China, becoming a hong (*xing*), a term still used in China today when referring to important companies.

Mennie produced several albums of reproductions of his photographs under the imprint of Kelly & Walsh, a leading bookseller in those times in Shanghai and Hong Kong. The remarkable album of photographs reproduced in this book appeared first in the volume *The Pageant of Peking*, published in 1920. Typical of the lavish approach to printing at that period, the photographs were reproduced in photogravure, in which the negative is used to make a printing plate in place of the accepted screen process, providing a much finer result. Mennie's other books – *Glimpses of China, Picturesque China, China North and South* and *The Grandeur of the Gorges* – appeared in the decade and a half from 1915. Curiously enough, for a man well-known in his day, doubt remains as to whether he was of British or American origin.

Mennie's work is remarkably modern in that it focuses not only on the great sights of Peking but on groups of ordinary people and their activities, in a manner comparable to the work of modern photographers. His photographs of Peking's architectural grandeur and its people going about their business are all the more remarkable given the technical limitations of both cameras and photographic emulsions with which he was working.

If Donald Mennie was called an 'amateur' photographer, this was only because photography was not his life-work. In any sober consideration of his pictures of Peking and its surroundings his stature is undoubtedly that of a considerable artist.

Mennie was interned by the Japanese when they invaded China and reportedly died in a Japanese prison camp at the end of the war.

A city as old as Peking gathers around itself a venerable air. Like some aged sage, the city that has been for so long the capital of a great country, of a grand civilization, takes on its own particular grandeur, a kind of innate nobility; and an outward tranquility.

On the surface, and some considerable way deeper down, that was the atmosphere, the general feeling of most visitors to Peking, certainly until the end of the nineteenth century, and even after the last of the long succession of Chinese dynasties had stumbled to its end and the Republic was proclaimed in 1912. For perhaps a decade after 1920 when the remarkable photographs in this volume were taken, the antique face of the city persisted, not only in its physical structure, which was resistant to change, but in the temper of its streets, its institutions, and in its social and other customs. The sudden reality of the end of centuries of imperial rule from the Forbidden City, standing red-walled and yellow-roofed in the city's midst, took some time to sink in. Throughout Peking's time as capital of the last two dynasties – a period of about five hundred years – emperors had wielded sole power in every department of life, power which was parceled out in small precisely designated areas to a huge number of state-appointed officials in descending order, from the highest mandarin down to the humblest provincial functionary. The structure of power was pyramidal. Once the emperor was removed, the entire structure of power's implementation ceased to have a controlling motivation. For a time, each official became his own emperor.

In real terms, not only in the capital but throughout China, everything which had been exclusively for imperial use, whether official or merely for the emperor's pleasure, gradually lost its semi-sacred nature and ceased to be forbidden to the populace at large. Slowly, with great caution, even trepidation, the several temples formerly used by the emperor and parts of the pleasure grounds adjoining the Imperial Palace were opened to the public. Yet the common feeling, product of age-old practice, that whatever had appertained to the emperor was still semi-sacred, took time to change. For years after the Republic took over, Peking Chinese were left, passengers in a rudderless boat. The new and completely unprecedented aura of a Republic took an equal period to be accepted.

The physical structure of Peking, its broad design, was formed in the Ming dynasty, beginning in the reign of its third emperor, the great Yongle (1402-1424). A city had existed on the site for centuries, however, and Yongle followed the general layout of the preceding Mongol city which was called Dadu (Great Capital) that he found when he moved to the city he made his capital. This Mongol city had been one of the world's great metropolises since at least the end of the 13th century when it was known as Khanbalic, (City of the Khan). In 1368 the Mongols were defeated by the forces of the Ming, which established its first capital to the south at Nanjing. The court and the capital were relocated under Yongle, and the capital city was renamed Beijing (Northern Capital) in 1421, romanized in the West as Peking.

This new capital city was laid out in a strictly controlled plan which in some degree reflected the square shape of the former Khanbalic, but not exactly on the same site. The outer walls of this square city, sometimes called the City of Nine Gates, were built to last and to exclude attacking forces. Constructed of rubble confined on either side by stone or brick facing, their structure at ground level was described by one later writer, presumably a New Yorker, to be 'as wide as Fifth Avenue'. Rising to a uniform height of about fifty feet with solid buttresses at intervals on the outer aspect, the walls were pierced at points symmetrically by huge gates, each topped by a pavilion-like, often triple-roofed structure to house the garrison. Along the top of the walls ran a broad path, allowing communication all round the vast area inside. The nine imposing gates were sited, two in the north wall, two each in east and west walls and three in the southern. The central southern gate was named Da Chianmen, the (Great Front Door), and from its high terrace the whole square area named the Tartar City, since it stood in part on the site of its Mongol predecessor, could be seen. Looking north from that terrace in 1920, it was still possible to see how, within the outer walls, lay two more rectangular enclosures – the Imperial City, forbidden to all except the emperor and the highest of his officials; and within that enclosure another, placed at its very centre, was the Forbidden City, sometimes popularly referred to as The Great Within. There, and in every other imperial construction, the roofs and walls were topped by golden yellow tile.

Standing on the terrace of Chianmen, at your feet a broad road runs north into a square at whose further end the red-walled, gold-tile topped Tiananmen, (Gate of Heaven's Peace) which is the Imperial Palace's high and commanding front door.

Beyond it, within the wide area, lies the rectangular sea of seven or eight golden waves which are the principal pavilions of the palace, flanked by other similarly roofed smaller buildings. The vista ends at the small five-crested rise called Prospect Hill, a delicate pavilion perched on each of its crests. The hill was made from earth removed in digging the wide moat that surrounds the outer walls of the palace. Facing the hill the northern palace gate, named the Gate of Military Prowess, is that from which the last powerless Ming emperor fled as the invading hordes murdered his family. Across a road the despairing emperor dashed to the bottom of the hill and hanged himself from a tree – the irony complete. In 1920 when the photographer of the pictures in this book was recording Peking, Prospect Hill was still closed to the public. It was opened in 1928.

Surrounding the palace enclosure was the much larger Imperial City, its walls still intact in the first few years after the birth of the Republic. The large eastern section of it was the pleasure ground of the emperor, his family and highest officials, a bosky parkland in which three small lakes were formed at the direction of the Yongle emperor in the early 15th century and were called 'seas'. Perhaps the best description of this former garden comes from one of the books on Peking by Juliet Bredon. The only child of an English father who was an official of the Chinese Maritime Customs, and his American wife, Juliet Bredon was born in China and lived there almost all of her life, mostly in Peking. She married Frenchman Charles Lauru who was an official of the Salt Revenue Department of the Chinese government stationed in Peking. 'As soon as we pass through the gateway [from the Forbidden City, writes Bredon in her book *Peking*] a radiant vista stretches before us. At our feet lies Nan Hai, the Southern Sea, with the Fairy Island of Ying Tai (Ocean Terrace) floating on it; and beyond the stately Western Palace roofs shining in the sunlight…. Like the builders of Versailles, the Ming knew instinctively how to compose a landscape. They understood the charm and surprise of contrast… appreciated the value of artificial water – a characteristic shared by all Chinese whose very word for landscape is a composite of hill and water – *shan sui*'. The emperor enlarged the existing pools… into the Three Seas, southern, middle and northern, and thereafter all the small palatial buildings near and around them were called Sea Palaces. 'Around the east shore of Nan Hai,' according to Bredon, 'runs a paved walk with small artificial hillocks from which, rumour says, the empress dowager Cixi watched the fires in the city on the dreadful night of 13 June 1900, when an allied [Western] army invaded Peking. Close by are the state barges. The empress was so fond of water excursions that she once gave orders to stop the bombardment of the [foreign] legations during the invasion in order to enjoy her picnic undisturbed by the noise of the guns.'

Bredon continues: 'Under a gnarled wisteria vine that… has braved the winds and snows and answered joyously to the first call of spring, our road leads on to the Empress Dowager's private theatre, built over water… to soften the voices of the actors.' Only one foreign-style building lies within this *rus in urbe*. Cixi treated it with disdain. The first time she opened her private apartments to receive ladies of the Diplomatic Corps their manners [apparently they fingered the draperies and curios] appalled her. 'Henceforth,' says Bredon, 'she ordered, these clumsy barbarians shall be entertained in their own vulgar surroundings.' Their next audience with Cixi took place in the Western-style building. The third of the Seas, Peihai, also boasts an island on whose summit rises a *chorten*, or Tibetan reliquary, a shape like some enormous white-painted bottle, with a gilded filigree cone for its stopper. It was built in 1652 to honour the first visit of the Dalai Lama to Peking.

The dragon coils of the Great Wall snaked across northern China to defend the Han people and their civilization from the Barbarian hordes. Still one of the most massive physical accomplishments of the human race, this redoubtable barrier proved daunting but never entirely impenetrable. It evolved from the separate and lesser walls of hitherto independent states that were finally brought into unity by Emperor Qin Shihuang, to fend off invasion. This section at Nankou Pass, north of Peking, classically illustrates the serpentine contours of its 6,700-kilometre length.

PEKING

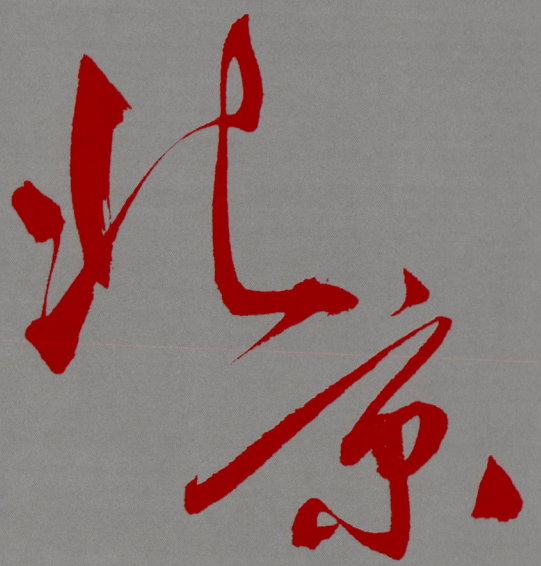

Constructed entirely of huge marble blocks, and dating from 1345, the Chu Yongguan, or Marble Gate, penetrates the Great Wall at the Nankou Pass near Peking. The keystone of the huge arch displays a garuda flanked by two seven-headed nagas whose tails disappear in foliage. The inner walls are partly covered with inscriptions made by various attempting invaders in their own languages – Tibetan, Mongol, Sanscrit, Uighur – some of them defaced by later rivals.

According to legend, several hours walk to the west of Peking there existed a pool surrounded by a thousand oak trees where there lived two dragons. The animals disappeared when the Monastery of the Oak Pool, Dan Zhie Si, was built but twin serpents took their place, small in size and confined in a red lacquer box.

When the emperor Qianlong paid a visit he was shown the box and told the legend. Unimpressed, he disputed the story of the serpent's supernatural powers. Over the years a whole number of religious buildings rose around the Oak Pool Monastery, making the site the largest and perhaps finest temple grouping in the Western Hills.

A grand pailou *stands at the threshold of the Thirteen Tombs – Shisanling – of Ming emperors set in the rolling slopes of the Western Hills outside Peking. Through its portals the Sacred Way leads onwards, and along this path the coffin of each emperor was ceremoniously transported to the chosen auspicious site for burial in its lavish underground chamber. On the way the procession passed between six pairs of life-size stone figures of*

animals, both real and mythological, and then between six pairs high officials. Among the animal figures in this curious guard of honour are lions, mythical xiechi, *camels, horses, unicorns and great sturdy elephants. Perhaps the nearest equivalent in royal cemeteries is the Valley of the Kings at Luxor in Egypt where the Pharaohs were put to rest in similar luxury subterranean chambers.*

In this deceptively simple-looking photograph a moment at one of Peking's gates is captured by the camera. Entering the city the donkey-cart and its passive driver are followed closely by what is probably a child carrying the two baskets of his load on a shoulder pole: a pedestrian approaches, with his hands full while people in the background have just entered the arch as another outside crosses the road: a small branch of a tree breaks the hard line of a building. The viewer is instantly there, involved in the moment of time and place.

The principal entrance to the Ta Cheng Miao Confucian Temple was through this monumental three-arch pailou *with its profusion of decorative tiles. The temple itself had been rebuilt many times and stood on the site of the original 13th century construction, next door to the Lama Temple at the north wall of Peking. Millions of Chinese Buddhists or Daoists also profess their adherance to the principles of Confucius as applied to the secular aspects of living. They do so without in any way diminishing their belief in one or other of the original Buddhist or Daoist religious faiths.*

The Yong Dingmen, or Gate of Eternity, was the southernmost portal on the long north-south line bisecting the rigidly planned concept of the city of Peking. The main gate with its tower (right) was itself enclosed within a semicircular wall fronted by a

smaller gate and tower (left). A nearby stream was convenient for personal or household washing. A single telegraph pole, peering over a low wall (left), provides the only clue that this scene was not captured in the Ming dynasty.

Outside the north wall of the Imperial City, on the north-south central line, the great hulk of the Drum Tower rises above the one-storey level of most other structures. Together with its partner, the smaller Bell Tower, these towers formed part of the Mongol city and were rebuilt by the indefatigable emperor Yongle when he built Ming Peking. Initially both towers told the time, the drum of one sounding the hours, and the clamour of the great bell in the other announcing various other important times – such as the hour for closing all the city gates in the evening. The bell kept time with the help of a

---

Moving the capital from Nanjing to Peking effected a profound change in the means of transportation. Camel trains, totally unsuited to haulage in the Yangtze basin, at once became the prime means of transport for both goods and people. The Bactrian camel, native of the deserts of central Asia, proved the ideal animal for the dry and dusty roads in and out of Peking. Its loud hoarse cry at the heavy loads strappod between its twin humps was a common protest heard on the busy highways.

clepsydra, a water-pouring mechanism that filled a large container marked vertically at hour-intervals. The first water clock was nicknamed by Peking residents, the Brass Thirsty Bird after the sculptured bird from whose golden beak the water poured. The combined noisy performance of the two towers lasted into the days of the Republic.

Further away, on the northern city wall lie the deep blue-roofed Lama Temple and the Hall of the Classics, the former once the boyhood home of the prince who later became the Emperor Yongzheng in the early 18th century. Its function as home to one who later reigned as emperor dictated its fate and it was turned into a temple since no commoner might inhabit the semi-sacred site where an emperor spent his childhood.

All those great buildings seen in the 1920's from the high terrace of Chianmen rose, yellow- and blue-roofed, well above the uniform sea of grey-roofed hutung dwellings of the common people, within the enclosing square of the city's walls. 'The moral effect,' says Juliet Bredon, 'on those who dwell there is curious. Strangers are impressed painfully at first with a sense of imprisonment. But in time this gives way to a soothing sense of security – to the comfortable sensation that the massive great arms of the city walls can keep out the rush and worries of the outer world.' Standing on Chianmen, she describes the scene: 'Because of the vast sweeping lines of the palace roofs these look even larger than they are. Their yellow tiles shining against the dark background of the Western Hills remain the supreme memory of the city – a picture changing, yet ever beautiful, beneath every caprice of hour and light.'

From a site on the eastern wall, Bredon describes a scene, still a memorable experience today: 'The day ends in a glowing brilliance with the western sky all fever-red. The violet masses of the hills... which form a background in all views of Peking... assume the aspect of loved and familiar friends. Then, as the light fades, their outlines soften. They seem to withdraw, little by little... almost regretfully into the shadows. One by one the monuments of the city, palaces... temples follow their example until, last of all, the gate towers and the walls themselves dissolve into greyness, and it is dark.'

So much for the Tartar (or Inner) City which, seen in plan, sits like a cube on the cushion of the Chinese (or Outer) City. To the south from the vantage point of Chianmen, this second portion of Peking, walled like the first, was yet one more product of the emperor Yongle's active, intelligent mind. Finding in his time that unauthorized suburbs were spreading beyond the south wall of the Tartar City and posing a threat to law and order, he enclosed the whole area, boxing it in, extending the imperial jurisdiction there, and equipping it with eight new gates. The existing three gates of the Tartar City's south wall now also served as gates in the new enclosure's north wall. It was in this way in the early 15th century that the capital city of Peking took on what was to be its final, definitive shape.

South from Chianmen, a large park dominates the eastern part of the view, and the dominant object within the park is the Temple of Heaven. It takes the shape of a traditional Chinese symbol, the *chu-i*, a sceptre-like object given as a token of good wishes to a friend, and composed of three circular shapes linked by a common stem. The temple mimics the *chu-i*, three round forms linked from north to south by a raised paved road or broad corridor. The French writer Claude Roy recorded his sensation on approaching it for the first time. 'You come to a great park,' with lines of ancient cedars. 'In the grass you will find violets and wild blue flowers. A long vista bordered with cypresses, paved like the ancient Roman roads, joins the Temple to the Altar.' Built in 1429, the Hall of Prayer for Harvests stands thirty-nine metres high, and was destroyed by fire in 1889 – just thirty years before Roy visited its successor. The original circular temple, with its massive triple blue-tiled roofs, had been supported on four huge lacquered columns of Chinese chestnut wood, 'painted with motifs of acid green, bright blue and gleaming gold – the centre of the ceiling a dragon on a blue background.' When, the temple was being rebuilt the Chinese architects discovered that there were no more Chinese chestnut trees of adequate size, and the new structure had to be supported on trunks of Oregon pine imported from the United States.

'At the far [southern] end of the great paved way,' Claude Roy continues, 'is the Altar of Heaven. In Chinese villages a worn stone cylinder stands in the centre of the square – the millstone. Here, then, is the great central Millstone, the polished pivot of Empire, dazzling, lustral, blind – a white mirror to the glaring light of day.' The Altar's huge flat circular platform of naked stone is placed atop three layers of balustraded white stone steps. Here, once a year the emperor came, after three days in the adjacent Hall of Abstinence, he mounted the loneliest place in all China. Here at the centre of that cold white disc, he prostrated himself and assumed responsibility for all the sins of the Chinese before Shangde, the Supreme Lord of Heaven.

When Claude Roy was contemplating the Hall of Prayer for Harvests, surely one of the most perfect buildings in all China, standing on top of three nine-stepped terraces in all its lacquered and blue-tiled magnificence, he relates how the temple guardian was there jotting down the impressions of foreign visitors in his notebook. 'I remarked that the proportions were so perfect that one could not displace a single balustrade without destroying the harmony of the whole. The guardian nodded... gravely. "The poet Po Juyi [742-846AD]", he told me, "once wrote of a very beautiful woman:

So perfect is the beauty of her body,
That the gods themselves could not add
Or subtract from her figure the thickness of a nail."

'I tried to imagine the guardians of Versailles quoting Racine to the visitors,' remarked the astonished Roy, when I told him this.

In the 1880s the Temple of Heaven was the Mecca of distinguished visitors in Peking. The prolific writer Mrs. C.F. Gordon-Cumming, described by one contemporary as a 'determined globe-trotter,' but whose accounts of her visit to China are generally accurate, tells in her book *Wanderings in China*, the story of an escorted official visit to the temple. The American Minister to China had arranged with the authorities for a certain General Grant and his party to visit the temple on an agreed date, provided no ladies were included in the group. Not to be outdone,

Mrs. Cumming with a resident of Peking named Dr Edkins decided they and several friends – some of them women – would visit the temple on that day, but somewhat earlier than the official party. When Mrs. Cumming's group arrived at the site the temple officials, expecting the authorized party, admitted them without question. The fate of General Grant's party when they arrived at the temple later, is not recorded by the triumphant Mrs. Cumming. General Grant, as perhaps Mrs. Cumming and her intrusive party may not have known, was none other than a former president of the United States and had been the commander of the Union Army in the United States' civil war. Her's was a victory over no mean foe!

A later visitor, during the early 1930s when restrictions had been relaxed, was an American, George N. Kates, the son of a Polish immigrant to the United States who became a successful industrialist. His son George studied architecture at Columbia University, and was fluent in several European languages. Reading widely in translations of Chinese poetry, he went to live in Peking and there studied Chinese, discovering what he called, 'the glowing wonder of a pure new joy.' In Peking he lived in a traditional Chinese house which belonged to a eunuch of the former imperial court. In his eight years in Peking he became deeply engrossed in all that was great in Chinese history, language and life, and when the Japanese overran North China he reluctantly returned to the United States and wrote the story of his life in Peking, which he entitled, *The Years That Were Fat: Peking 1933-1940*. One among a multitude of Chinese subjects which Kates discusses in his book is the surprisingly early establishment of the capital city's definitive shape. 'Of all the cities of the great world none can rival Peking, for the regularity and harmony of its plan. As a design it reflects the social scheme that called it into being. And although that scheme has now slipped forever into the past, so powerful and enduring was its expression in terms of space and enclosure, of axis and perspective, that a curious illusion is produced.... All the citizens of Peking, Chinese or foreign, are conscious of the city's majesty; the sheer breadth of the setting enhances composure and lends dignity to everyday manners.

'The plan,' Kates writes 'is composed about a single straight line drawn north and south through the centre.... The massive surrounding walls are so regular, except for a single bend at the northwest corner... that if one were to fold a map along that line, the east and west sections would very nearly match. Along this riving line formerly went all authority in the capital, for... squarely upon it, stood the Forbidden City.... The power of a whole empire had once radiated from this central cell.' Kates goes on: 'Peking', with its night-shut gates and impregnable walls, moated and guarded, 'had to be set in proper relation to the whole world about, even to the planets.... Orientation, once complete, was to achieve no less than a harmony between man and nature.... The Temple of the Sun was set outside the walls to the east, that of the Moon exactly to the west, opposite. The Temple of Heaven in the south was balanced across the main axis by the Temple of Agriculture. As one moves about within and without the metropolis, sun and moon, heaven and earth are thus constantly in mind. This is one of the charms of Peking.... If architecture influences men unconsciously, is it no wonder that the inhabitants of such a city were more enlightened, more truly cultivated than those of any other in China? If one enquires concerning almost any amenity one will hear in conversation: "In Peking they arrange it thus." That is the criterion.'

Kates was also struck by the formal pattern of the boulevards and broad avenues 'that ran almost from wall to wall, especially the long straight ones running north-south in the Tartar city. Two chief avenues pierced through the residential quarters either side of the palace. At the intersection... with similar ones

running east and west were triumphal Chinese arches with brightly painted wooden framing supporting high banks of glazed coloured tile. These were the *pailou*. A single such arch in the east and west cities marked the crossings at the level of the outer courts of the Forbidden City. A hollow square of four arches was erected at more northerly intersections of the main boulevards. These four points, East and West Single Arches and East and West Four Arches, were centres for commerce and trade in the city.' Kates quotes the Chinese teacher who wanted to have a silver band fitted to his new tobacco pipe, as saying: "I must go to that good silversmith's at the East Four Arches." And another friend told him that he had heard, "there will be a great silk sale tomorrow at the new shop about to open near West Single Arch." '
When a native of Peking becomes nostalgic, says Kates, 'he is not thinking of the Great Within or some splendid temple courtyard: more likely he is longing for the savour of the brisk trade, the crush of prosperous crowds amid the cheerful babble of native voices somewhere near one of the familiar *pailou*. Here rickshaw boys must *walk* their vehicles; here if one glimpses a friend, one must salute promptly before he is borne past on the milling stream. This is Chinese urban happiness!'

For himself, Kates 'had selected a much quieter

part of the town to live in, north of the palace. 'To it, I was later told, most serious Western scholars eventually moved.... The neighbourhood was... congenial. There, the half-deserted former palace properties were magnificent, tall trees spreading over long unbroken stretches of high wall in the tranquil lanes.... There were many unpretentious houses like my own.... In time, I came to distinguish quite clearly, as did all true Pekingese, between the manners, almost the accent, of my own part of town and places as little distant as the East and West Single Arches. In early summer... there were hours when one could hear the insects buzzing in the linden trees, against a background of silence like that of a small country town. The vendors of refreshments settled comfortably under their blue cloth canopies for the long day... unhurried. Conversation was more tranquil, voices melodious. Life here flowed traditionally; this was my part of town. "So let me live," said the farmer poet Tao Yuanming, over fifteen hundred years ago, "thus should I be content to live and die, and without questionings of the heart gladly accept the will of Heaven." '

Claude Roy, who lived in a different part of Peking, describes the action there. 'In my sleep I know it is half past six because the noodle merchant's rattle is going, *cra-cra-cra*. Between two creaks comes his cry on four notes: *la,mi,la,mi: Jieh mian! Jieh mian!* A quarter of an hour later it is the sesame cake vendor beating a three-four rhythm on a hardwood tablet hanging from the bamboo pole on his shoulder; then his nasal cry rings out: *Chao ping! Chao ping!* Between five minutes to and five minutes past seven, the vegetable merchant appears; a bunch of long copper stalks attached to his tray echoes the rhythm of his footsteps with an occasional capricious *dling-dling*. He announces his wares of the day in a triumphant tone: Cabbages, celery, salted turnip leaves, boiled sweet potatoes, spinach, lotus roots, French beans, marrows. At a quarter past seven you may as well give up trying to sleep. The *huang zhiang* (bean sauce) merchant comes round the corner of Smiling Patriarch Street and Duck Skin Alley blowing his old French regimental bugle.'

In the midst of a largely featureless plain, Peking rose up like some mirage in the eyes if the traveller. It's cliff-like ramparts were designed to awe and intimidate, giving due warning to all who came that they must 'tremble and obey,' as an imperial edict put it, the orderly behaviour of those privileged to walk its streets. Something of the force and scale of Peking's majesty as the imperial capital is innate in this scene of a heavily laden cart, its struggling horse assisted by a mule, approaching Yong Dingmen, the Gate of Eternity, in the city's southern wall.

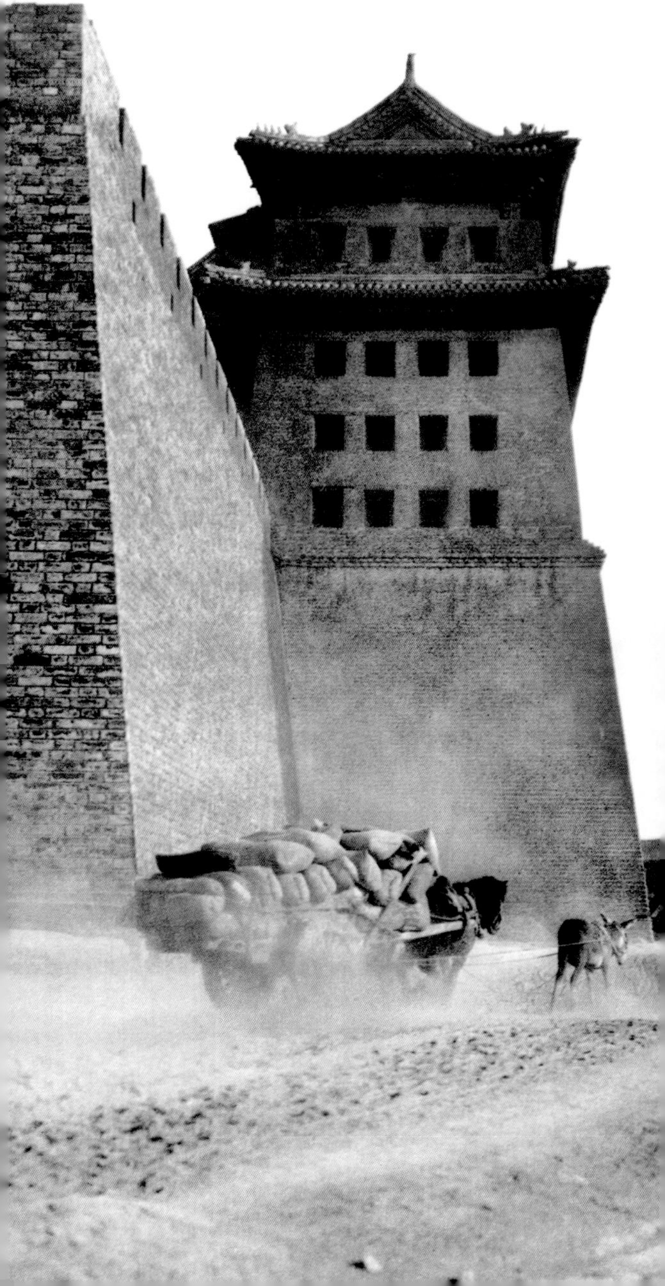

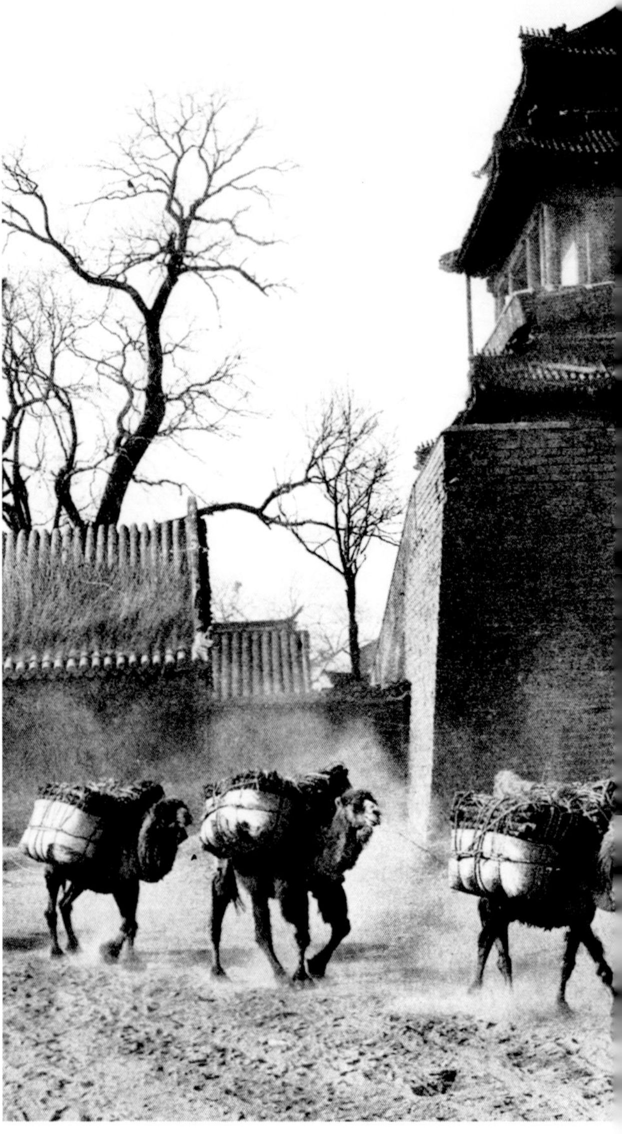

It is winter. Bird's nests perch in the bare trees outside one of Peking's gates. A camel train with its master approaches the city wall, each beast laden with heavy packs. Throughout history the camel was the main carrier of goods of all kinds from coal to warm the houses, building materials, rice and every other material needed in large quantities.

Peking's generally rainless summer and its proximity to large desert areas is uncomfortably punctuated by fierce dust storms. From the dry heat under a blue sky, within a few minutes a wind springs up and the air is saturated with grit to the extent that visibility is

often nil, or at most a few yards. Here the donkey acts as pilot to the horse struggling in the shafts of a hugely overloaded cart. A few yards to the rear another transport team is scarcely visible through the heavy clouds of dust and sand.

Ta Chianmen, Peking's Great Front Gate, centrally placed on the southern wall dividing the Tartar from the Chinese City, towers far over the heads of the working people. In imperial years the central portal remained tight shut at all times except for once in the year when it opened to admit the emperor's procession on its way south to the Temple of Heaven to take on his prayerful shoulders the sins of the Chinese people. By 1920 the dark passage through stood open to the carts and rickshaws, workers with goods hitched on shoulder poles and ordinary pedestrians alike.

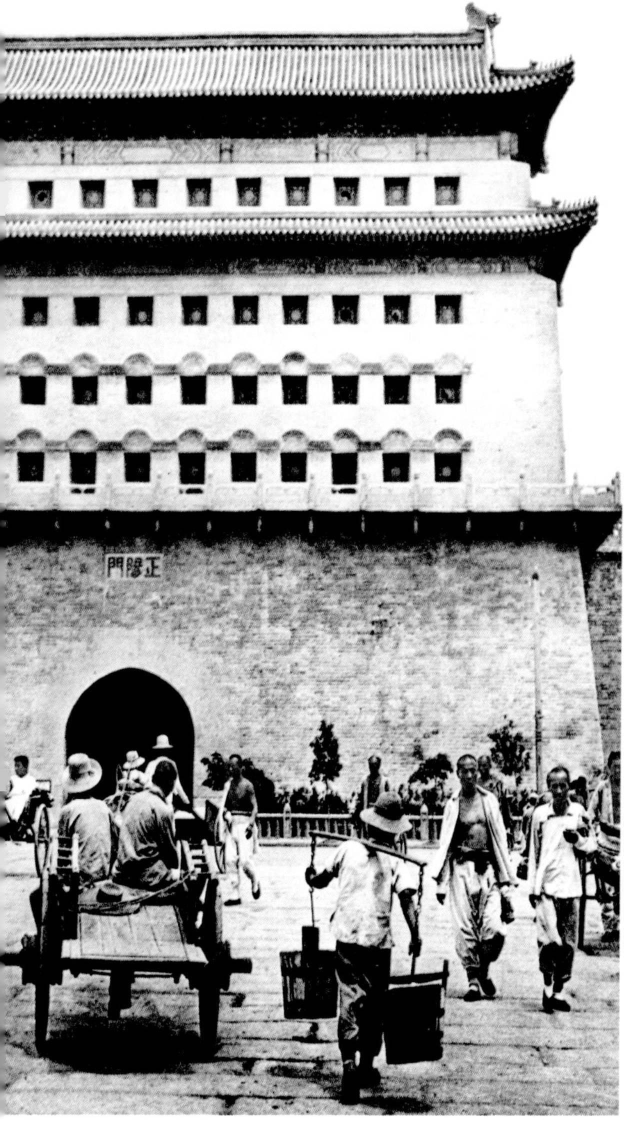
正陽門

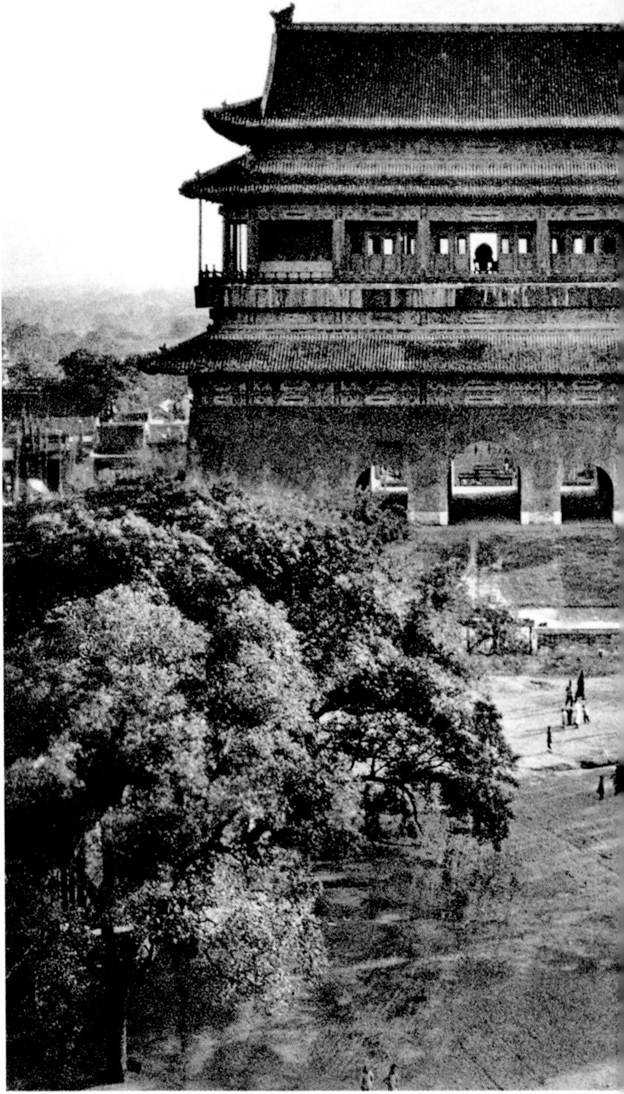

Rebuilt quite close to its original site in the early 15th century, the imposing Gulou or Drum Tower sounded on its drum the watches of the night. Here it was photographed from the adjacent Bell Tower, looking south. In spring and summer the cityscape of Peking, as its deciduous trees burst into green luxury, took on a park-like appearance, each building springing from surrounding trees.

Conveyances of every description, from donkeys, mules and camels to single-wheeled carts and covered wagons, passed through the portals of elaborate pailou, *the honorific arches that advertised the excellence of local commercial and industrial activity.*

The central lane was for wheeled traffic, while the width of the thoroughfare had to leave sufficient margin for parked vehicles, pedestrians and the storage of materials required by road-builders employed to improve the paved surface.

With their clutter of pots and braziers steaming in the morning sun, wayside food stalls were havens of rest and sustenance for Peking's workers and for travellers alike. In the capital's often icy winter they could be

uncomfortably chilly places, but the winter air brought release from the heat and dust storms of the summer – and some hot food to warm the stomach.

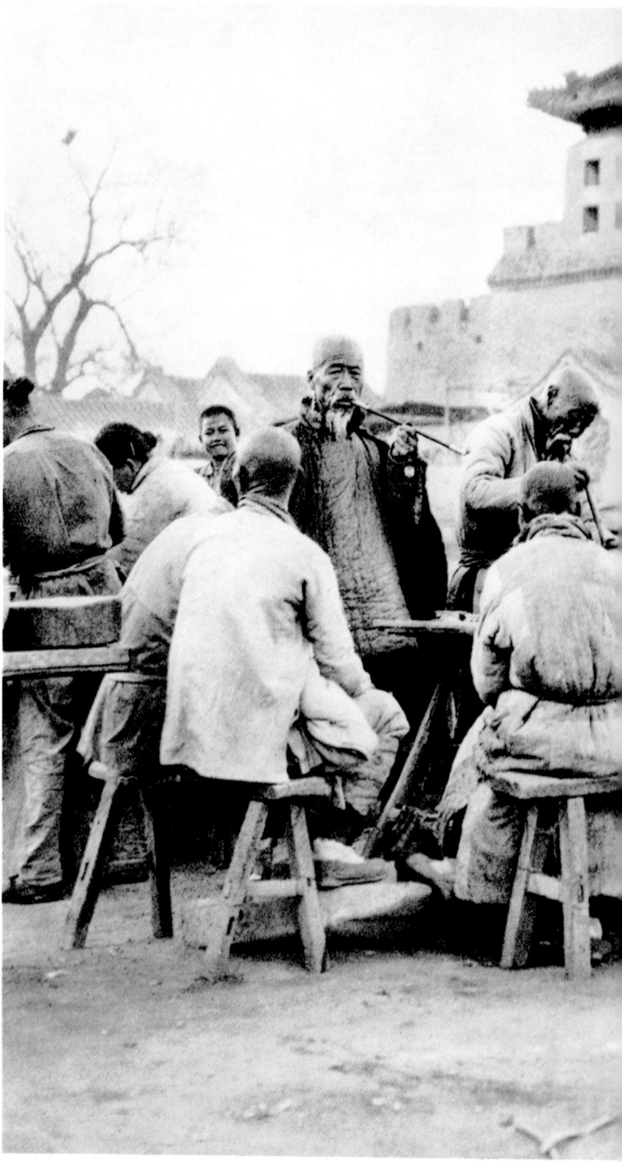

By the 1920s the pigtail, which all Chinese men were forced by the Manchu to grow in token of their submission to the non-Chinese rulers of the Qing, had mostly been cut off and shaven heads were common. This causal group of workers, wrapped thickly against the winter cold, takes a snack as they chatter to each other, some smoking the common long pipes with their small brass bowls. The stall holders, to the left, are busy preparing more food, one of the city's large gates perhaps offering a degree of shelter from the cold wind.

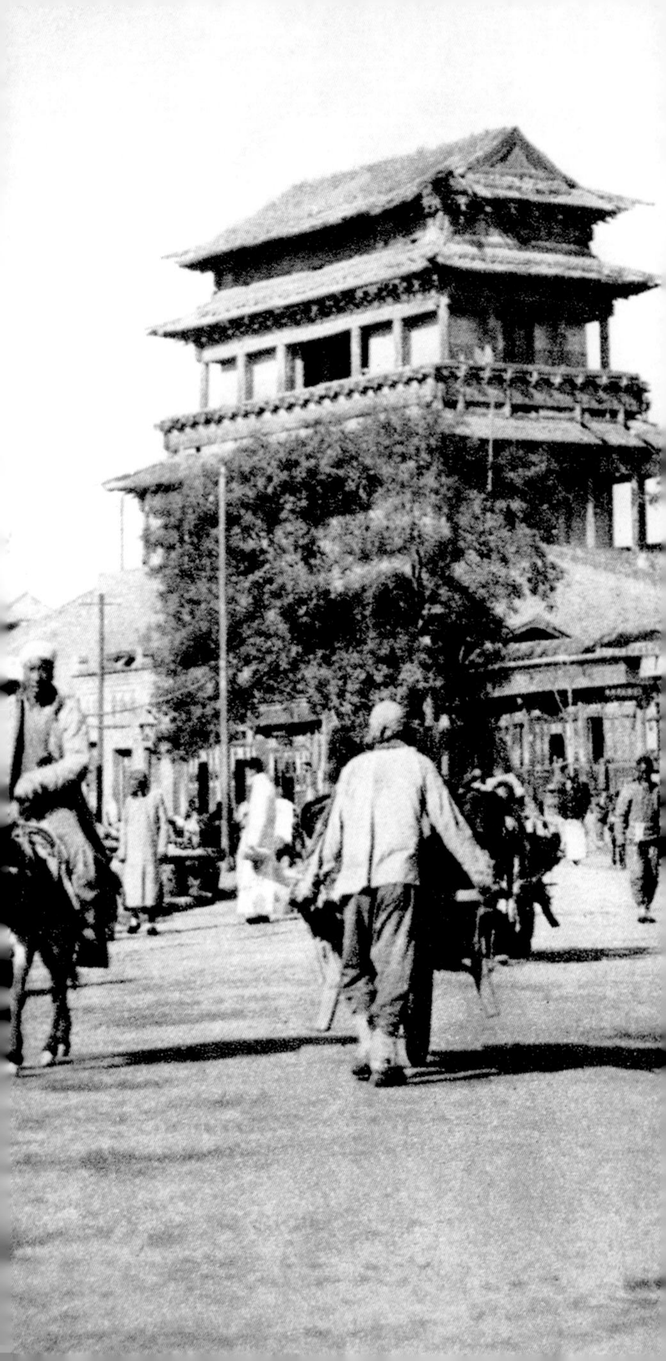

The pioneer photographer of the Orient, Edinburgh-born John Thomson without whose early photographs much of human and documentary interest would have vanished without visual trace, recounts many an encounter in Peking. On entering the city through one of the gates 'We pass through… in the wake of a train of camels laden with fuel from the coal-mines not far off. There is a great noise and confusion. Two streams, made up of carts, camels, donkeys and citizens have met beneath the arch [of the gate] and are struggling out of the darkness at

The name of this tall gate of the capital's north wall was correctly Desheng Men, literally the Gate of Victory, but local people called it the Fruit Gate since the whole immediate area consisted of shops selling fruit grown in the near countryside. One of the curious aspects of Chinese commerce in cities as well as in small towns, is the tendency of shops in the same line of business to occupy adjacent premises in one street, or in two adjacent streets. The business of selling fruit in Peking was conducted predominantly around the Fruit Gate.

either end. Within, there is a wide thoroughfare, by far the widest I encountered in any Chinese city, as roomy as the great roads of London.' Inside the city walls Thomson describes how a 'cartway runs down the centre of the road, and is only broad enough to allow two vehicles to pass abreast. The causeway in the middle is kept in repair with material that coolies ladle out from deep trenches or mudholes... on either side of it.'

Peking shops, Thomson discovered, 'were elaborately carved and painted, and gilded so beautifully that they look as if they ought to be set under glass cases, while their interiors, are fitted up and finished with equally scrupulous care, the owners ready for business inside, clothed in their silks, and looking a prosperous, supremely contented tribe.... Walking proved treacherous there... while shopkeepers spread out their wares for sale so as to monopolize at least two-thirds of the pavement.... Sometimes one can only get through the press by brushing against the dry dusty hides of a train of camels as they are being unladen before a coal-shed; and one must take care, should any of them be lying down, not to tread on their huge soft feet, for they can inflict a savage bite.'

Somerset Maugham, one of the English-speaking world's most renowned writers and playrights of the first half of the 20th century, was also fascinated by the city's unique shops. 'When you travel in China I think nothing surprises you more than the passion for decoration which possesses the Chinese.... Not just memorial arches [*pailou*] where the occasion for it is obvious, but on the common household items. The pewter pot is enriched with a graceful design; the coolie's bowl has its rough but not inelegant ornament. You may fancy the Chinese craftsman does not look upon an article as complete till by line or colour he has broken the plainness of a surface. But it is more unexpected when you see the elaborate embellishment of a shop-front, the splendid carving, gilt or relieved with gold, the intricate sculpture of its façade. It may be that this magnificence serves as an advertisement; but it does so only because the passer-by, the possible customer, takes pleasure in elegance'.

This was certainly true of traditional Peking shops which echoed designs from the past. Often, in fact, such establishments had no name or other sign outside to inform the passer-by of what their business consisted. Instead an elaborate decorative invention cloaked the façade, presumably, as Maugham thought, to charm, to lure the potential customer.

'Much of the entertainment of the city,' Thomson thought, 'centred in the streets... there are peep-shows, jugglers, lottery men, ballad singers and story-tellers.... The story-teller, however, has many competitors to contend with, and of all his rivals the old-clothes men are perhaps the most formidable tribe. These old-clothes men enjoy a wide celebrity for their humorous stories, and will run off a rhyme to suit the garments as they offer them to the highest bidder. Each coat is thus invested with a miraculous history which gives it at once a priceless value. "It was this fur [Thomson is quoting the old-clothes hawker] which, during the year of the great frost, saved the head of the illustrious family Chang. The cold was so intense that people were mute. When they spoke, their words froze, and hung from their lips. Men's ears congealed and were devoid of feeling so that when they shook their heads they fell off. Men froze to the streets and died in thousands; but as for Chang of honoured memory, he put on this coat and it brought summer to his blood. How much you say for it?"'

Thomson had the rare opportunity of meeting educated Chinese. Among them was a Mr Yang, a member of the Public Works Board, who invited Thomson to his home. Thomson explains that this was an unusual gesture because Chinese seldom admit strangers into the inner court of their dwellings, for these they hold to be sacred and inviolate.... 'I enjoyed exceptional advantages for gleaning information about the inner life of the wealthy Chinese classes... and their households, inasmuch as I never let slip the opportunity of volunteering to take family portraits.'

Another resident of Peking in the first half of the 20th century was Harold Acton, whose book *Memoirs of an Aesthete* typified English writing of the 1930s on the subject. Born of a moneyed family, he was brought up in the family house La Pietra, a few miles from Florence, and cultivated an intense interest in things Chinese. Self-taught in its literature, especially its poetry, and in its civilization, he arrived on the coast of northern China on a boat from Japan and from there went on by land to Peking. 'I did not have to kiss the soil of this long-promised land, for it rose in eddies to kiss me; it filled my mouth and eyes and nostrils; my teeth gritted against it. Fine particles of China's venerable earth were blown along with me all the way to Peking. A thin yellow haze hovered over the mounds of graves which outnumbered everything else on the horizon. It was one vast cemetery, and the houses of the living were not very different – cubes instead of mounds.

An immense calm descended on me as in the Roman Campagna. I felt strangely at home….' He had arrived in one of Peking's famed dust storms as daunting for the traveller as the capital's heat and humidity in summer.

'An attendant in a grubby gown brought me some pale tea to wash down the dust, and a steaming towel to freshen my face, which felt wizened, as if I were a mummy newly risen from one of those mounds on the plain. I sat back and admired the beauty of the landscape where life and death were so closely intermingled. The earth looked tired with aeons of cultivation, yet here and there it yielded a fresh green down, and clumps of willows drooping in delicate thought. I had been waiting for years to see this country,' Acton goes on. 'My imagination, nurtured on Chinese history and art…' – on Arthur Waley's translations of Chinese poems… on Chuang Tzu and the Liao Chi…. 'Thus, though I had not studied the Chinese language, I was tolerably equipped for my visit.' He quotes the great English historian Edward Gibbon, author of the *History of the Decline and Fall of the Roman Empire*, who said that on reaching Rome the Eternal City he had to wait several days "before I could descend to the cool and minute investigation." ' Acton had no such feelings. He set out at once for the Imperial Palace.

'Neither Versailles, nor the Pitti, nor any palaces I had seen, with the exception of the Vatican, had the magnificence of this extensive city of open courtyards and pavilions. Within our time no handiwork of man has achieved such a dignified and spacious harmony of buildings.... For once the sky was part of the architectural design. The sweeping curves of the golden roofs held the blue sky like jewelled chalices. Massive though the buildings were... they had an aerial lightness and grace. Instead of clamping them down to earth, the roofs helped them soar.... Apart from a few guards and custodians dwarfed by the latitude and longitude of the buildings, there was no sign of human life. The Olympus, whence China had been governed, was as deserted as a pyramid in the desert.'

Acton studied Chinese at Peking National University, and was asked to teach a course on English composition. 'Here was an opportunity to deal with something tangible, to sow the seed and watch it sprout. During classes we read and analysed passages of English prose, and alternatively I would give a general theme and let the students write on what they pleased.... [Then] I would criticize each in turn explaining my corrections and suggesting appropriate models and exercises.... I devoted two afternoons a week to these tutorials and was dazzled by the results. What English undergraduate could express himself in as lucid and fluent Chinese?.... The fourth-year students were less interesting than those in the third year. They made fewer grammatical errors, but many had crystalized into purveyors of mild platitude coated with saccharine. They had a sense of balance derived from classical Chinese prose, but having mastered an adequate vocabulary they surrendered themselves to automatic writing.

'When I considered the poverty and future prospects of most of my students... I admired them for being so cheerful. Their pleasures were simple and scanty, but they extracted the utmost enjoyment from them. This zest for life was sharpened by a keen consciousness of the rhythm of nature, a deep sentiment of man's harmony with the universe.' Acton quotes several passages from the students' writing in illustration. It seemed to him that they got 'more from life than our [Western] wealthier undergraduates. There were surprises, of course: "Imagination is a charming, lithe linnet that exists in the region Incognito and usually flits from bush to bush invisible to the naked eye." My students,' Acton was surprise to discover, 'were cheerful until they took up a pen. The liveliest of them [then] would be invaded by melancholy during the process of composition.... "Melancholy thoughts seized upon me," was a recurring cliché.' And Acton quotes one example from a student who writes a description of a young boy lost to the world and rejected by life – lachrymose in its self-conscious intensity, ending: "I wished to suffer in order to know life more clearly."

The English writer of that classic traveller's tale, *Escape With Me*, describes with delight a Peking experience for which he was unprepared. Osbert Sitwell, was the most animated and reactive of the famed Sitwell trio. Soon after he arrived in Peking, he became aware, while writing by a window in his *hutung* house, of 'an intermittent music that floated down from the sky and drew me out into the court to see what it could be.' High up against the blue dome of the sky a flock of birds was manoeuvering. 'When the creatures sped in a straight line the music came low and regular... but with each turn in their flight it grew... stronger and seemed to contain a note... of menace such as I had heard in no bird-song heretofore.' The birds were too high up to be identifiable and he thought it strange that their fluting should be loudest during their circlings and loopings. 'Could it be due to the pleasure, perhaps, which they took in their evolutions?'

At this moment his houseboy appeared: 'Master

not heard pigeons make whistle music before?' Master had indeed not, nor had anyone mentioned how the Chinese 'tie whistles to the legs of the pigeons, or how a boy carrying a flag which... the birds were able to identify, runs along to indicate the line of their passage to keep them aloft as long as their owner wishes.' Sitwell turns to Chinese writer Dun Liqen's *Annual Customs and Festivals in Peking* where the subject is marvelously and intricately described. The whistles are attached to the tails of the birds. Large and smaller models are the most common. But three pipes clamped together, or five or eleven, or even thirteen double pipes – and so on, in a bewildering variety to produce "an equally various melody. When the pigeons wheel overhead, their sound rises even to the clouds," writes Dun Liqen, "containing within it all five notes [of the Chinese scale],"

'In former years,' Sitwell discovers from the same Chinese source, 'some of them were taught to steal. They were trained to fly, directly they were set loose, straight to the Imperial Granaries and swallow as much of the finest rice as their crops, artificially distended, would receive.' Returning home, they were dosed with alum and water and made literally to disgorge their booty. After being washed, the rice would then be sold. The proprietors counted on a flock of a hundred pigeons bringing home fifty pounds of rice a day. 'How clearly,' Sitwell comments, 'has this device been invented by the same race which evolved the ingenious use of the cormorant for fishing!'

Harold Acton had gone to the Great Wall at the invitation of his third year students and had an enjoyable spring day there. Osbert Sitwell mentions the Wall, but it apparently aroused no special feelings in him, for he accords it only a few lines. But the Great Wall of China had been a subject of wonder, even astonishment in Western circles almost from the construction under the rule of the First Emperor two thousand years ago. C.P. Fitzgerald, great historian of China, describes it accurately and without exaggeration. 'This stupendous fortification following the crests of precipitous mountains, scaling the steepest slopes, curving and winding among the barren hills of north China for hundreds of miles.' Even today when the traveller first catches sight of that portion not far from Peking it is hard to take in the fact that it was built entirely by uncounted hundreds of thousands of men with little but the most elementary of tools. The astounding ease with which it streams up and over great mountains, curves down again and with a grand sweep as deft as that of some giant serpent takes off into the distance, is one of the most breath-taking experiences in the world. Its value as a defensive fortification must never be underestimated. Professor Fitzgerald, a cultural historian, rightly qualifies this by describing the Wall's major disadvantage. It could only be effective if garrisoned along virtually its whole immense length: and, running as it does for great lengths through scantily populated and impoverished countryside, it was never easy to maintain and replenish that garrison. The consensus today among historians sees the Great Wall as much more of a cultural barrier, preserving Chinese society and its language from corruption by the spectrum of Central Asian languages, and thereby saving the unique qualities of Chinese society.

One of the main arteries of Peking, Antingmen Street ran due south from the gate of that name in the city's northern wall, bearing a ceaseless flow of carts, palanquins, rickshaws, water-carriers and pedestrians, interspersed with the occasional caravan train and funeral procession. Antingmen Street, together with Hatamen Street to its east, were the two largest and busiest thoroughfares on the eastern side of Peking.

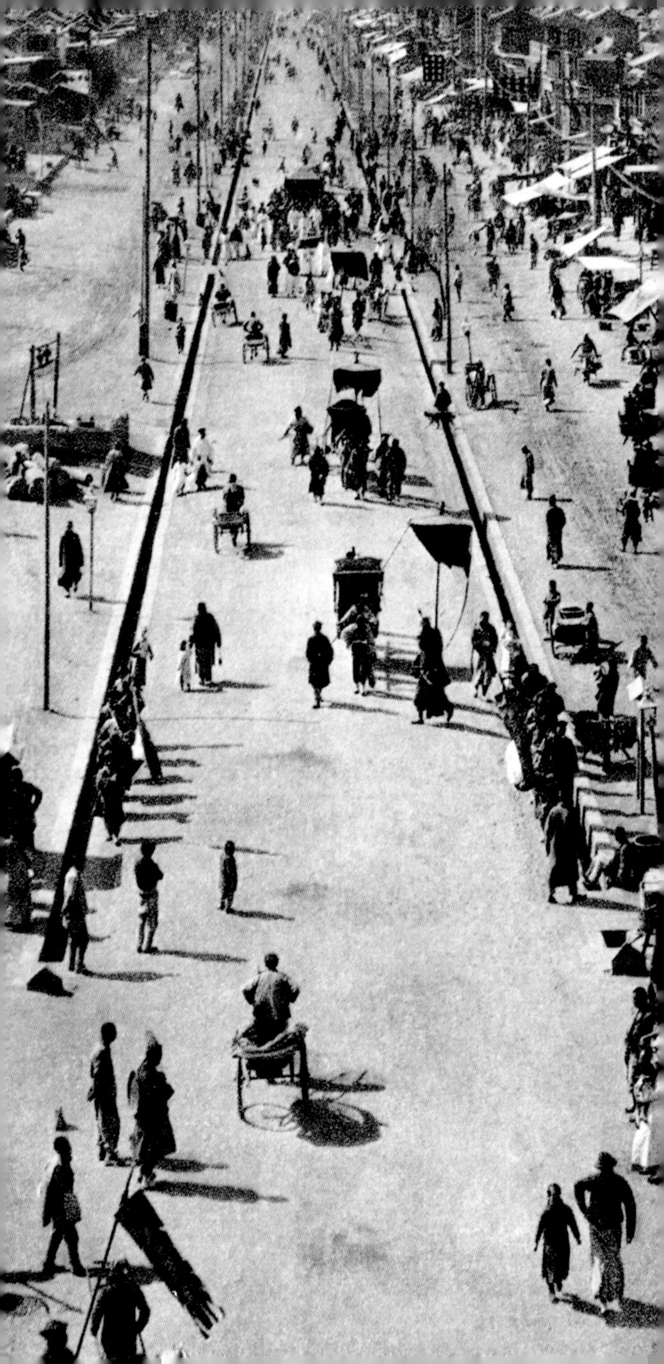

Arriving in the streets of Peking, this camel caravan may well have travelled the fabled leagues of the legendary Silk Road, bearing teas, spices, medicinal curiosities or perhaps nothing more exotic than sacks of grain. A four-thousand-mile network of interconnecting

trails that bridged China and India to the Near East and the verges of Europe, the Silk Road crisscrossed the Eurasian continent and shaped the course of both Asian and European history and culture.

Most visitors to Peking remarked in their writings on the astonishingly lavish decoration of shop-fronts. Encrustations of elaborate wooden panelling seemed excessive for a store which, at first sight, appeared to

deal in baskets and other household utensils. Obviously such florid decoration was designed to attract customers, but at a cost that would seem out of proportion to the relatively small profit margins of such an enterprise.

A more elegantly dignified restraint is evident in the decoration of this establishment, which betrays no outward clue to the nature of the business conducted within. While emperors still ruled China, they alone

could decree construction of buildings in the capital that were more than one storey high. The city's planning regulations were designed to ensure the Son of Heaven's transcendence over all.

The courtyard of the Yong He Kong or Lama Temple is situated at the end of Hatamen Street on the northern wall of the Tartar City. The buildings were the boyhood home of the Yong Zheng emperor (1723-1735) who, on his accession to the imperial throne, donated the complex to the Lama priesthood, since custom forbade any other use for a building that had been home to one who later ascended the dragon throne. The most famous sight of the temple is the tall gilded Buddha of the Resurrection (Maitreya) carved from Yunnan cedar. The figure is 23 metres tall – the Lamas measure height otherwise and say he is 23 elbows tall.

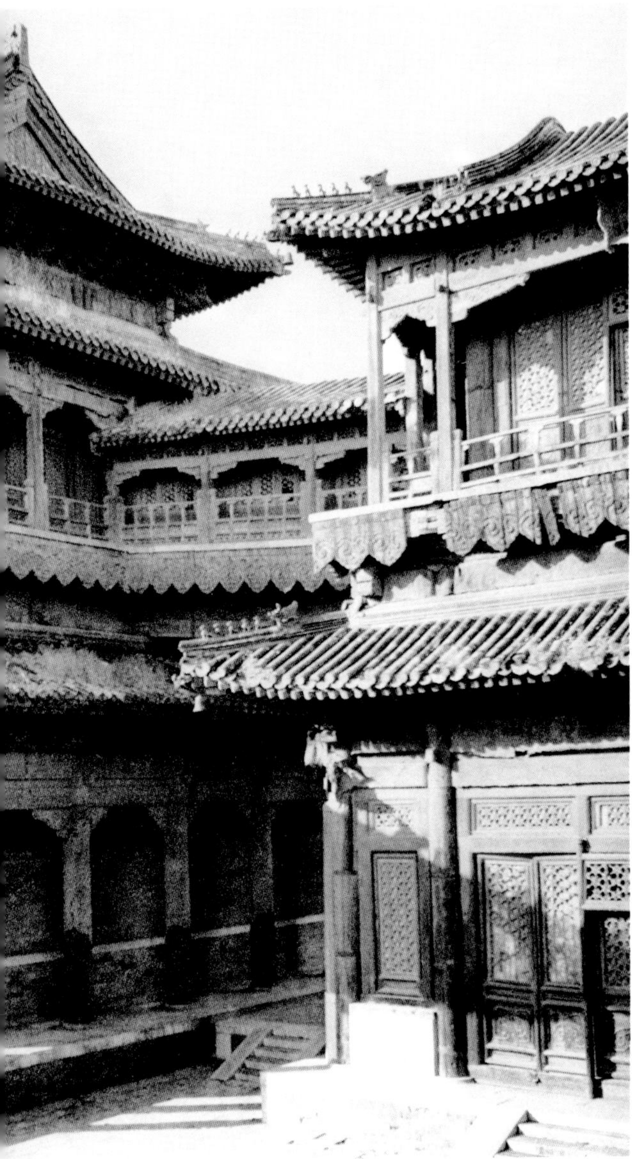

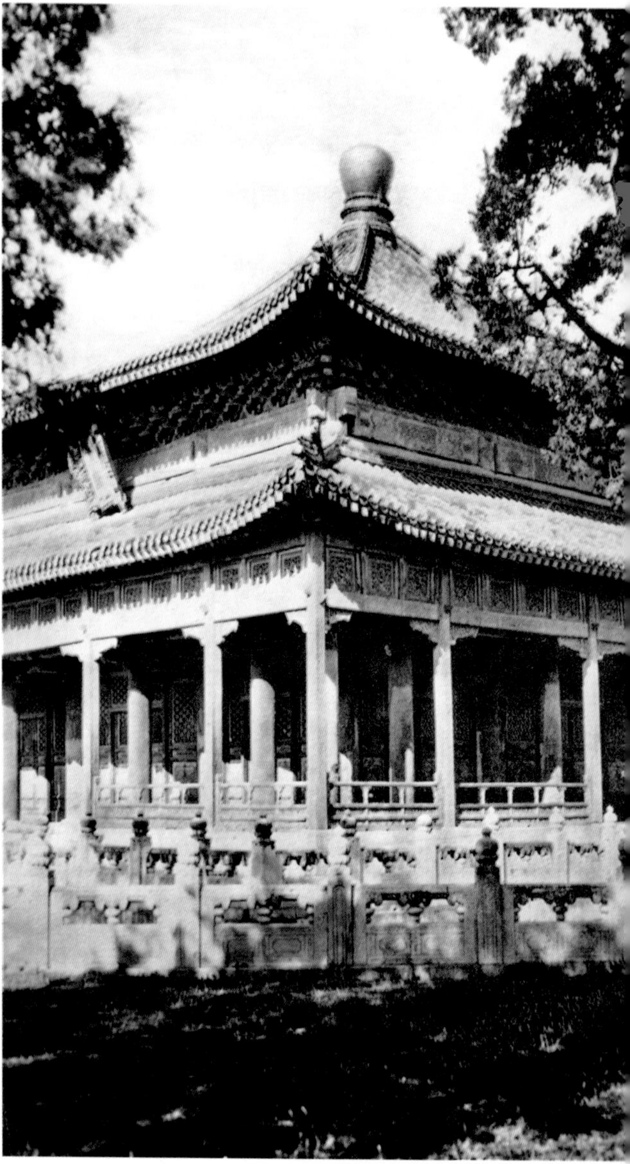

Adjoining the Lama Temple, the Hall of Classics (Gou Ci Jian) was built on an ancient site in the centre of a circular pool. In its galleries the texts of much ancient Chinese literature, including the teachings of Confucius, were engraved on stone slabs. These slabs were arranged in page-like forms convenient for copying by means of stone rubbings. In dynastic times such classics, whose length was about half a millian characters, had to be learned by heart by would-be scholars. The Hall of the Classics is approached through a pailou *of great dignity and elegance.*

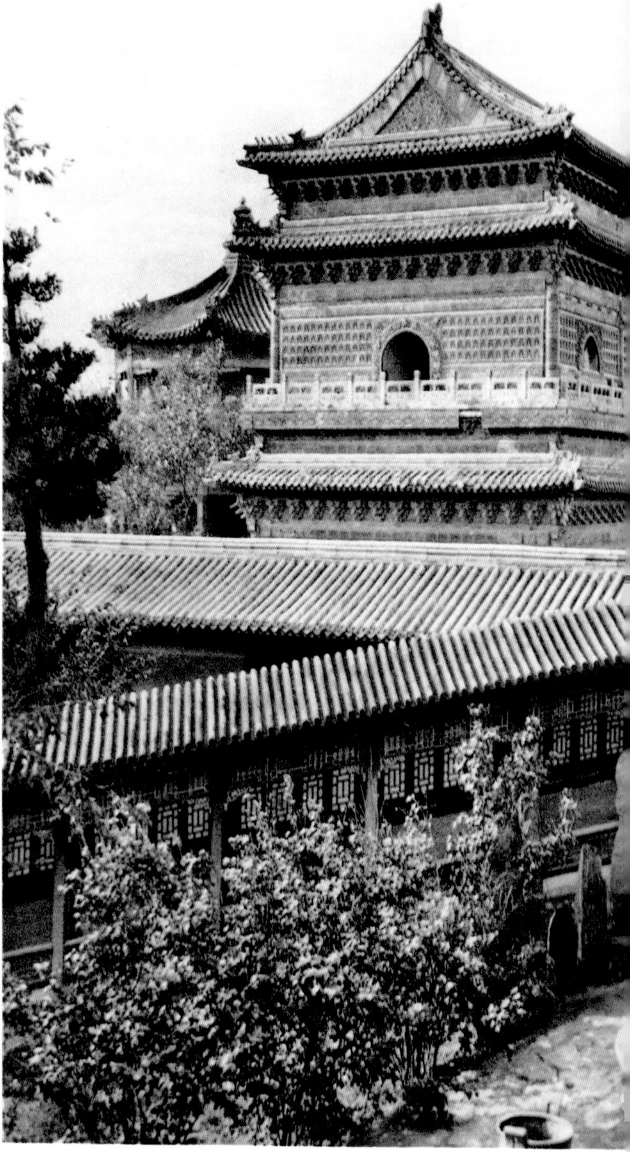

Among the many temples in the rural paradise of the Western Hills one of the outstanding examples is the Monastery of Ten Thousand Buddhas (Wo Fo Si) with its statue of the sleeping Buddha. The figure is fifteen metres long, clothed in robes of state, and wears a serene expression described as 'an embodiment of dreamless sleep'. The figure is carved from a single trunk of sandalwood. In the adjoining pavilions are niches designed to accommodate ten thousand gilded Amitaya Buddhas, many of which were looted when Allied forces in 1900 were attempting to crush the Boxer Rebels.

Another of the famous sites in the Western Hills is the Monastery of Azure Clouds, Bi Yin Si. Dating from the 12th century, it was twice restored and enlarged by two of the palace eunuchs who planned, unsuccessfully, to have their graves set on the auspicious hills just behind it. Many buildings are located around those of

the Temple, overlooked by the Diamond Throne Pagoda atop the hill. Dating from 1792, and with a spectacular view, the pagoda was inspired by a model of a Buddhist temple in Bodhgaya, India, which had been given to the Imperial Court early in the 15th century.

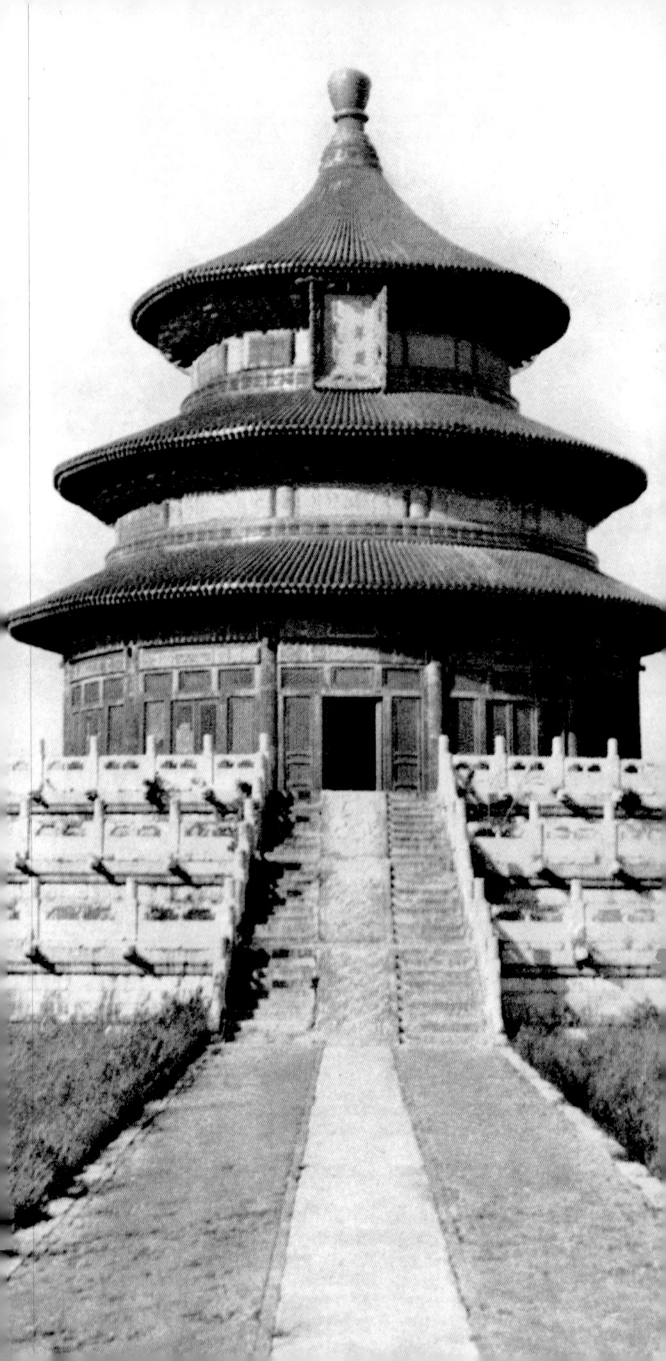

Perhaps the best account of that part of the Wall near Peking, among many others dating from the latter part of the 19th and the early 20th century foreign residents and visitors to old Peking can be found in Juliet Bredon's *Peking*. 'The classic excursion from Peking which no tourist should omit, even if only in the capital for a few days, is to the Great Wall at the Nankou Pass. There are many other places where the Wall may be seen... as it stretches for

---

Once a year, on the day of the winter solstice, the emperor with his entourage visited the Temple of Heaven complex in the Chinese City. There he worshipped, praying to the Shangti, the Lord of the Universe, and taking on his own shoulders the sins of the whole Chinese people at the Altar of Heaven, the southernmost of the three elements of the Temple. At the left stands the great Hall of Prayer for Harvests with its triple blue-tiled roofs, set on great circular platforms, each balustraded with carved marble. The emperor prayed on the single plain disc of the Altar of Heaven – a site that has been called 'the loneliest place in all China'. The ceremony first took place in the Zhou dynasty (1100-771BC), and the last recorded person to perform the rites was General Yuan Shikai, the first president of the Republic of China on 23 December, 1914.

nearly 2,000 miles from the coast at Shanhaikuan to the borders of Tibet. But nowhere is… it in better, preservation, nowhere grander than at Nankou Pass,' about 25 miles from Peking by train. 'The quaint old town [of Nankou] is the first link in the chain of defenses built across the narrow defile beyond to keep back the Tartars. A short distance above the town, the hills gather and we come to the entrance to the gorge guarded by four watchtowers. This is the spot where, according to Chinese poets, the visitor should muse at sunset, when the light falling upon the Kingfisher coloured rocks, is one of the eight sights of the neighbourhood. Only the brush of a great artist,' Bredon herself muses, 'could reproduce the scene: the narrow entrance to the wild and rugged pass, water- and wind-worn, lying in darkness as if blotted out with ink; the crests of its grim walls slowly turning from flame to sapphire, then to most intense violet – the foreground tinted with delicate purples and blues. The journey to the Wall at the top of the pass may be made by train. How prosaic, the stranger exclaims, to view such a renowned sight from a [railway] car window!

'As the engine slowly puffs up the narrow valley, the steep, bare hills rise higher… and passengers disembark at the Bright Dragon Bridge. Thence it is an easy walk… along the old highway to the Pa Ta Ling (Great Wall Gate)… at 2,000 feet above sea level.... The Wall crosses the pass here, and through a massive archway a magnificent view opens up of the plains of Chili and the distant snow-capped mountains.... On either side the Wall wanders along the crests of scaling peaks which it seems impossible even the foot of man could climb.... Not a soul to be seen save for our donkey driver who has tied his beast to an old cannon lying in the grass.'

The expedition ends with a visit to the Languages Gate through the Wall. Built in 1345, it is constructed of massive marble blocks. Within its passageway the stone bears inscriptions in six languages: Chinese, Mongol, Syriac, Tibetan, Sanskrit, and Tangut. Most have been damaged, doubtless by the writers of rival language inscriptions, but there is one more inscription carved by the restorers in 1445, and a plaque of Qing date describing the gate as 'The First Fortress of the World.' Considering the passage of time and event since 1922 when Juliet Bredon wrote her book, nothing much has changed.

There is one subject on which travellers both Western and Chinese seem to be unanimous – the rustic charms of the Western Hills close to Peking. Given the strategic importance of this barrier, and the occupation of the site of Peking long before it was the capital, it is hardly surprising that some of the finest temples and monasteries in all China should have been built there.

Mrs. Hope Danby, long resident in Peking, wrote a book, *My Boy Chang*, both interesting and entertaining in its social comment on Westerners and Chinese in the capital in the early decades of the 20th century. 'How hot it is, I grumbled one afternoon in June to Wang who was serving tea in the courtyard [of her *hutung* house]. I can scarcely breathe – a week in the hills would be like heaven just now.' Wang replied: "It belong fine weather – but time not suitable." Not suitable? What do you mean? "Many soldiers walkee all time" said Wang. I gazed up at the sky. It was of the palest blue, cloudless and clear as tourmaline, and the slanting sun had turned the courtyard into a pool of stifling heat. It must be lovely and cool, though, at my favourite temple in the Western Hills, I thought longingly. Indeed, I seemed to hear the soothing tinkling of the bells as they swayed in the breeze under the eaves of the shrines; it decided me at once to go there.'

It was common at that time among Westerners and others in Peking to reserve accommodation in one or other of the temples in the Hills as a retreat from the city's summer heat. Mrs. Danby's retreat was in the Monastery of the Sleeping Buddha, one of the oldest in the Western Hills, the original dating from the Tang dynasty. 'The soldiers won't bother me. I'll go the day after tomorrow.' She told Chang to hire a car, and that he must come with her. 'We'll make an early start….

'The sun was already blazing when I dressed in country slacks and a silk shirt that sparked and crackled with electricity as I drew it over my head. A great deal of noise was coming from the front door. When I went there, I gazed with amazement at the sight of the rickety old car – it was like a bulging, gorged elephant with all the paraphernalia tied on to it which Chang thought necessary....

'I didn't interfere, because nearly everything was already secured to the roof and running boards with ropes. Chang, beaming with pleasure, importantly ordered the chauffeur about, and... we were off in a swirl of dust, with the five beggars and other *hutung* people bowing farewell at the gate. It took some time to pass through the city; one had to proceed slowly with much tooting of the horn because of absent-minded, seemingly stone-deaf pedestrians who wandered inconsequentially in the middle of the streets. But at last we went through the West Straight Gate (Xi Zhi Men) at the northwest corner of the Tartar City wall and were on the Great Stone Road to the Summer Palace and the hills.

'Nothing delighted me more than my trips to the Western Hills. I even enjoyed bumping along the road which was paved with uneven blocks of granite. Chang, sitting proudly in front with his pet lark in its cage, turned every now and then to point out the sights.' But Hope Danby's eyes were always on the road itself, its users a glimpse into the medieval ages; 'invariably there were priests and pilgrims on their way to the temples; jolly innkeepers setting out food under matsheds; farmers with their buxom wives following a few paces behind; and the itinerant sellers of every imaginable thing from needles to crockery. The letter-writers under the shade trees dozing as they waited for clients, the mobile barbers, shoemakers and others.... Surely the Pilgrims' Way to Canterbury must have looked like this in Chaucer's time? Later, came a group of actors, some on stilts and all laughing merrily as they made their way back to Peking.

'At last we came to the fine, dignified avenue of dark cypresses that led to the entrance of the temple. There we were met by an old friend, one of the Buddhist priests, who was waiting for us. I dare say that he hoped that I had not forgotten to bring my usual offering of cherry brandy and crème de menthe which he and the Abbot enjoyed so much.'

Mrs Danby settled in her pavilion on a high rockery with its gold-tiled, gold-tipped roof. The emperor Qianlong, who began his rule in 1736, so loved this temple where he occasionally rested that he wrote an inscription for a stone tablet extolling its perfections. It was still there, moss-covered but readable.

'I was at peace here... and the world with its constant anxieties had receded into nothingness.

avoided, and the Court passed many months in a purpose-built country retreat which was frequently improved. In those times the Chinese passion for gardens was at its height and numbers of Western Jesuits were employed in lay-out and architecture, resulting in a fine rustic pleasure-ground, many of whose official buildings had a European flavour.

In 1860, Anglo-French armies invaded China and captured Peking. The Yuanmingyuan was set ablaze and almost all of it destroyed. A young officer the British army Royal Engineers named Charles Gordon, found himself appointed to the expeditionary forces sent to China in the effort to combat the Taiping rebels. Gordon was posted to Peking, when he and his comrades found themselves at the mercy of the Dowager Empress who tried to use the force against the rampaging Taipings in an effort to save the Peking Palaces. Later, however, by another quirk of fate, the expeditionary forces were ironically ordered to attack and destroy one of the very palaces, the Yuanmingyuan, which they had earlier protected. Gordon went on to become leader of the expeditionary force, earning the nickname 'Chinese Gordon.' But his reaction to the sack of the Summer Palace was far from happy: 'We went in [to the Summer Palace] after pillaging and burning the whole place.... It made one's heart sore to burn [the palaces]. The army was in such a hurry that

A kind of trance came over me – it was the famous spell that bemused the residents of Peking and which the French called the *microbe de Pékin*. With a sigh of contentment I set about unpacking my things.'

Unconsciously, perhaps, Hope Danby echoes a theme found very often in Chinese poetry. The poet Wang Wei of the 7th century captures the essence in his short poem, Bamboo Grove Retreat.

Alone among the close bamboos
I play my flute and hum my song
So softly not a soul will hear –
Except maybe old friend the bright moon....

Peking is spectacularly well endowed with places of interest – ranging from sites of historic significance to urban and rural beauty. In sight of many of the temples in the Western Hills, or from the roads to and from Peking, lie the two Summer Palaces, one in ruins, the other substantially rebuilt for the Empress Dowager.

The original Summer Palace – the Yuanmingyuan or Garden of Perfect Brightness – was built in the early 18th century by the emperor Yongzheng (reigned 1723-1735), and it was he who established a routine followed by later rulers in which the Court was moved from the Great Within after each Chinese New Year (in January or February), into the Yaunmingyuan where it remained until the Winter Festival, when it returned to the Great Within. In this way the worst of the summer heat of the city could be there had been no time to save any of its contents.'

The second Summer Palace, Yiheyuan – The Garden for Cultivating Harmony – had long been a favourite with the Court. The site, close to the first palace, is largely covered by the artificially created Kunming Lake which adds some beauty to the area.

Another young traveller, Peter Quenell, arrived in Peking when he was 26, escaping from his disillusionment over Tokyo, about which he seems to have harboured deep romantic delusions. He had gone to Japan to teach, imagining that his students would be an 'assembly of Zen monk scholars meditating on *tatami* mats.' In his book, *A Superficial Journey Through Tokyo and Peking*, alluding to the students of the 'Japanese miracle' of industrialization, he characterized them instead as worker-ants, and the atmosphere of Tokyo as 'airless and hard to breathe in as an old building filled with whirring modern machinery.' He left for Peking with a sigh of 'overwhelming relief.' He found China as different from Japan as he could have wished. He admired the Kunming Lake but felt the pavilions and the long covered walk in the Summer Palace that runs by one side of it, built about the middle of the last century, bore 'horrid witness to the depravity of Chinese taste.' Although arranged with a certain magnificence upon the hillside and a sense of symmetry, 'this serves merely to underline their tawdry unimaginative detail…. Walking through the courtyards... one might have been visiting some gimcrack Chinese fantasy conceived by the promoters of a World Fair. It was obvious as one entered the great pavilions, that the Empress Dowager's personal taste in bric-á-brac must, to an extraordinary degree, have coincided with that of the least enlightened English tourist.' And he goes on to note the increasing failure of Chinese taste in the later years of the Qing dynasty.

On the return journey from Yiheyuan to Peking, the singularly fine natural setting and attractive prospect of the country chosen as location for the Shisanling or Thirteen Tombs of the Ming Emperors, quickly efface any memories of the architecture of the Summer Palace. The first sight as you approach the tombs is a grand five-arched *pailou*, perhaps the finest of its kind in China, which dates from 1541. The size and the elegance of this gateway at once alert the visitor to what lies beyond and cannot yet be seen. The visitor next encounters the Great Red Gate, followed by the Tablet House with its giant stone tortoise, and then by the Spirit's Road to the Combined Mausolea and the Triumphal Way which extends for several hundred metres, lined by six pairs of standing and seated animals: lions, *xiechi* (mythical beasts), camels, elephants, horses and unicorns. These are followed by stone monolithic figures of scholars, administrators and warriors, and by the Dragon and the Phoenix Gate that leads to the wide view of softly rising ground interspersed with gentle valleys – the superb terrain of the Ming Shisanling.

Fittingly, the Chanling tomb of the emperor Yongle is the largest and most impressive of the Thirteen Tombs. Each tomb takes the form of all imperial structures in Peking, several buildings set as if in a single large courtyard, each with an earth tumulus and a stele tower. Beneath are the underground burial chambers. The great wooden hall of the Yongle tomb was constructed in 1427, and named the Great Hall of Sacrifice. It is probably the largest wooden building in the world: its 32 structural elements are of *nanmu* from China's southwestern forests. The illustrious Yongle was laid to rest within the enclave. One of China's most complete, agile and creative minds, a man of forceful personality – the creator of Ming China is hardly too strong an estimation of his achievements in its rejuvenation. His sixteen concubines joined him in separate chambers. In accord with ancient Chinese custom they were buried alive, a barbaric requirement of imperial protocol not discontinued until the reign of Hongzhi (1488-1505) when the women from then on were spared that terrible fate.

The Great Hall of Sacrifice secluded in its courtyard makes a statement of dignity and grandeur. The tiled-roof wooden building affirms a kind of sober beauty in form and style. The siting of the tombs, large and small, points to the Chinese eye for composition, with landscape of low hill and rolling valley forming a harmonious complement in shape and colour. Coming from the Summer Palace and its ill-used landscape, its tawdry detail, the achievement of the Thirteen Tombs is as astonishing and heart-warming as it is inescapable.

The Ming Tombs is yet another of the places portrayed by the talented photographer who beautifully captured the Peking he encountered and experienced so memorably in 1920. Over eighty years have passed since then, profound changes in the life and habits of the Chinese have deeply altered China, yet the monuments the Chinese created in their unique history in and around Peking still ring in the sight and memory with an unmistakable note.

When the Dowager Empress Cixi moved the administration to the Summer Palace in 1889, hiring over a hundred eunuch cooks and spending many millions of taels on her sixtieth birthday party, the extravagance of the Qing dynastic rule become apparent. Cixi's invention of a long corridor, its ceiling painted with birds and flowers and bordering the northern shores of the Kunming Lake, had no forerunner in Chinese architecture. Skirting the small hill whose top was crowned with the Temple of the Sea of Wisdom, it ended at another of the Empress's ridiculous inventions – a Marble Boat grounded on the shore and used for her picnic parties.

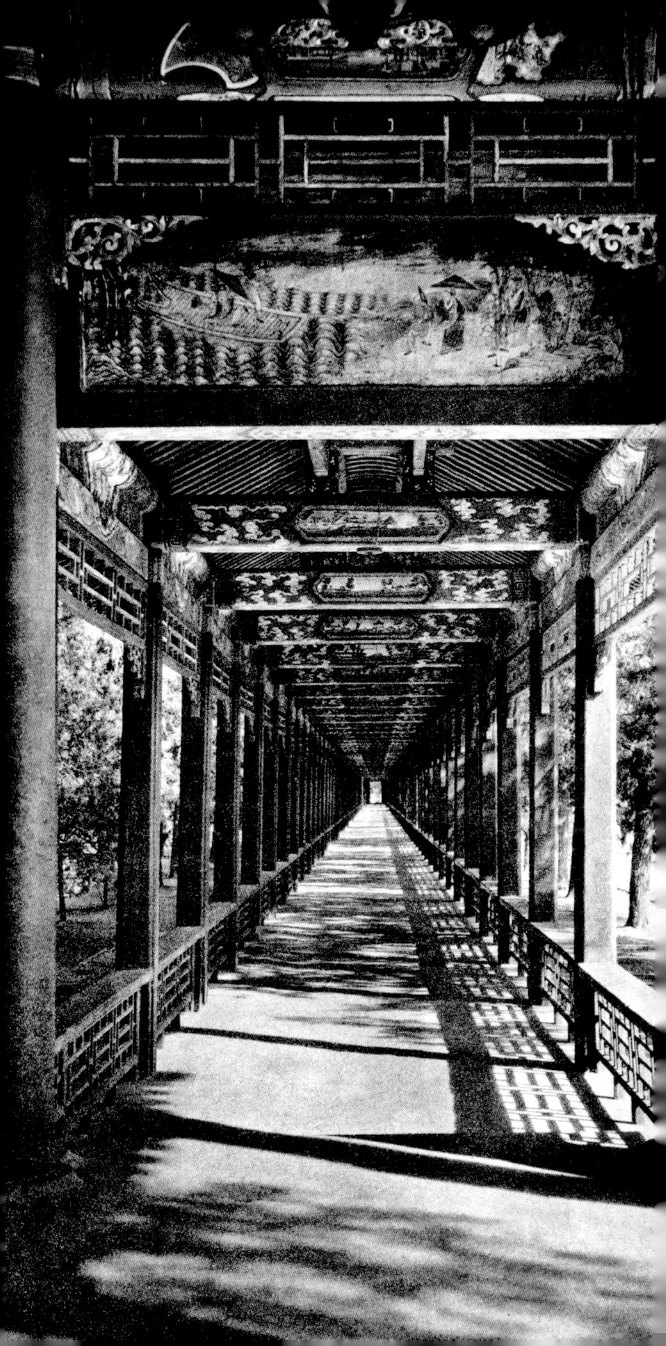

The ornately tiled and gabled structures on the slopes of Longevity Hill overlooked the north shore of Kunming Lake, and included the private quarters of the Empress, with views of the Western Hills in the distance. The history of the Summer Palace is tracable back to the Yuan Emperor Kublai Khan when he attempted to

improve Peking's water supply with the construction of canals from the hills to the Lake. Several hundred years later Qianlong (1736-1795) added lakeside gardens and a temple of Gratitude and Longevity in honour of his mother's birthday.

*The Seventeen-Arch Bridge from the western shore of
Kunming Lake led to a small island housing a
miniature temple. The extravagant structure of the
bridge underlines something seen in many forms in
China – the national delight in decoration. The
balustrades of the bridge are topped along both sides by*

scores of carved stone lions in many different poses, and at either end of the bridge larger carved lions terminated the balustrades. Chinese architects seem to have been particularly inspired by the presence of water and the need to transcend it with structures verging on the fanciful.

At the eastern end of Kunming Lake in the grounds of the Summer Palace this apparently eccentrically shaped bridge was so built for the purely practical purpose of permitting small sailing vessels to pass underneath. Its shape has led it to be endowed with various names: Camel-back Bridge, Hunchback

*Bridge, and even Jade Belt Bridge, this last for no
reason other than its proximity to the Jade Fountain.
The Chinese traditional joy at the sight of the full moon
reflected in still water was even more acute when
observed through the elegant window the bridge's arch.*

SOURCES OF QUOTATION

Juliet Bredon – Peking
Published by Kelly and Walsh Ltd. Shanghai. 1922
Pages: 21-22, 35, 85-86, 88, 89

Claude Roy – Into China
Translated by Mervyn Savill/Published by MacGibbon & Kee Ltd, London. 1922
Pages: 30, 33, 36-37

George N. Kates – The Years That Were Fat: Peking, 1933-1940
Published by OUP, Hong Kong. 1988
Pages: 69-73, 75

Somerset Maugham – On A Chinese Screen
Published by William Heinemann, London. 1922
Pages: 205-207

Harold Acton – Memoirs of an Aesthete
Published by Methuen & Co Ltd, London. 1948
Pages: 275, 276, 341, 343

Osbert Sitwell – Escape With Me. An Oriental Sketchbook
Published by MacMillan & Co Ltd, London. 1949
Pages: 189-191

Hope Danby – My Boy Chang
Published by Victor Gollancz Ltd, London. 1955
Pages: 80-83

John Thomson – A Window to the Orient
Published by Damson Low, London. 1875
Pages: 25-26 (Later appeared with other publishers)

Peter Quennell – A Superficial Journey Through Tokyo and Peking
Published by OUP, Hong Kong. 1986
Pages: (Introduction X), 201-202

C.F. Gordon-Cumming – Wanderings in China
Edinburgh & London, William Blackwood and Sons. 1900
Pages: 374-380